THE
LONDON
BUILDING WORLD
OF THE
EIGHTEEN-
SIXTIES

THIS IS THE FIFTH OF THE
WALTER NEURATH MEMORIAL LECTURES
WHICH ARE GIVEN ANNUALLY EACH SPRING ON
SUBJECTS REFLECTING THE INTERESTS OF
THE FOUNDER
OF THAMES AND HUDSON

THE DIRECTORS WISH TO EXPRESS
PARTICULAR GRATITUDE TO THE GOVERNORS AND
MASTER OF BIRKBECK COLLEGE,
UNIVERSITY OF LONDON,
FOR THEIR GRACIOUS SPONSORSHIP OF
THESE LECTURES

THE LONDON BUILDING WORLD

OF THE
EIGHTEEN-SIXTIES

JOHN
SUMMERSON

THAMES AND HUDSON
LONDON

Printed in Great Britain by Jarrold and Sons Ltd, Norwich
0 500 55005 0

When I was honoured with the invitation to give this lecture it was indicated to me that the subject should be one which would have pleased the late Walter Neurath. This opened many doors for I do not know what subjects might not, in one way or another, have intrigued him. One recalls what was so characteristic of him – his strong sense of inquiry, of getting inside a subject. As Nikolaus Pevsner said of him in introducing the first of these lectures in 1969, 'Walter Neurath did not confine himself to the obvious and saw very clearly the possibilities of the far from obvious' – to which I would add the possibility that there is sometimes more to the obvious than meets the eye. The subject I have chosen – building in mid-Victorian London – is, perhaps, in the present climate of opinion, a sufficiently obvious one and what meets the eye is not always pretty. I offer it, however, with the conviction that it is worth the kind of inquiry which Walter Neurath would himself have welcomed and encouraged.

1 Work on Holborn Viaduct nearing completion, July 1869.

IN THE SEVENTH DECADE of the nineteenth century, London was more excavated, more cut about, more rebuilt and more extended than at any time in its previous history. Consider the situation as Londoners of the time experienced it. Think first of the main drainage, with the deep trenches for four intercepting sewers ploughing across the town and its suburbs in long crazy zigzags from west to east, an operation continuing through all the ten years. Then the cut-and-cover work for the Metropolitan Railway, running the length of Marylebone Road and Euston Road, with the operations for the District Railway making more havoc as the two companies united in forging the Underground's inner circle. For the fifth great sewer and a superincumbent highway the Victoria Embankment was begun in 1862, but the southern stretch of the District got into it, too. Above ground, the main-line railways were forcing themselves into London. The Pimlico Bridge carried two companies' lines to Victoria in 1859; the double station and the portentous hotel opened in 1862. In 1864–66 two more railways crossed the Thames from the south. The South Eastern swung out from London Bridge and, with the help of seventeen bridges, a hundred and ninety brick arches and an iron viaduct, with the destruction of a hospital, the removal of eight thousand bodies from a graveyard and the construction of a new Thames bridge, got itself to Charing Cross. With less effort it lurched across the Thames into the great shed at Cannon Street. The LC and DR, meanwhile, drove north from Penge, crossed the river with yet another bridge at Blackfriars, paused at Ludgate Hill, then steamed on, across the very threshold of St Paul's, to Holborn. In the north, the North London struck down from Dalston and built the Broad Street terminus in 1865, while the Midland came grandly down through the Middlesex fields to a new station called St Pancras whose cathedral façade belongs to 1870. Nor was this all. New highways were grooved into the old street pattern. Victoria Street in 1860 was still a long, open scar. Garrick Street, cut in the fifties, was built up from 1861. Southwark Street started building in the following year and went on into the seventies. The ruthless Queen Victoria Street, pickaxing the City all the way from Blackfriars to the Mansion House, and carrying in its belly a main sewer, the District Railway and gas and water subways, was partly opened in 1869; while the City conducted its own adventurous bridging of the Fleet Valley, with Holborn Viaduct built in 1866, the new meat market of Smithfield in 1867–68 and the new Blackfriars Bridge in 1869.

These were the massive, crude constructional enterprises of the time. They accompanied and partly instigated a building and rebuilding of great richness and variety. For the City itself this was the critical decade of the residential exodus. In 1861 the City still had 113,000 inhabitants, in 1871 only 76,000. The old Stuart and Queen Anne mansions, long since deserted by their masters and made over to managing clerks, were giving way to strictly business buildings, offices or warehouses.[1] The breed of masters had gone to Bayswater or Kensington or perhaps to Hornsey or Clapham; now the breed of clerks was going to Camberwell or Peckham, Stoke Newington or Highbury. According to the District Surveyors' returns over 73,000 new structures were built in the metropolitan area in the decade, the majority being suburban dwellings.[2] But if it was a decade of sweeping change we must also remember the tracts that did not change: Bloomsbury and Islington, Marylebone and Mayfair, St James's and Belgravia. They remained almost as Georgian as ever so that, in spite of all, it can be said that in 1870 London was still the Georgian metropolis.

A great part of the scene I have just sketched came about through engineering enterprise, though there were architectural attachments at many points. In this paper I shall have nothing to say about engineering. The railway story has been superbly handled by Barker and Robbins[3] and if the history of 'improvement' above and below ground has yet to be written it is not something to which I will attempt a contribution here. I mean only to probe a little into the world of ordinary building where, year by year, architects, builders, surveyors and a host of tradesmen and labourers were constructing banks, offices, warehouses, hotels, theatres, music-halls, taverns, churches, chapels, schools, hospitals, orphanages, workhouses and all the other components of the London we call 'Victorian'.

The proportion of London's population concerned, in one way or another, with building was high. In 1861, the population of the capital was 2,800,000 and of these, according to the census returns, 91,000 were employed on 'houses and buildings'. Slightly more than 10 per cent of the male adult working population was so employed. The category is widely drawn for it includes house proprietors and house agents as well as architects, surveyors, builders and workers in all the building trades.[4] It includes – to name one trade only – 27,000 carpenters. Extracting the three most immediately responsible classes we have, in the 1861 returns, 3,845 builders, 1,459 architects and 749 surveyors.[5] These figures are grossly inflated as we shall see in a moment but, relatively to the national figures, they give us a striking measure of London's building capacity in relation to the rest of the country. Thus, London had 24 per cent of all builders in England and Wales, of architects 38 per cent and of surveyors 40 per cent. The ratios were not very different in 1871 – the same in respect of builders, but there had been a strong growth outside London in the profession of architect and still more in that of surveyor.[6]

The figures for people calling themselves builders in the census returns are misleading for reasons which may easily be guessed: any character with a set of tools doing some random jobbing could set himself down as such. Kelly's *Post Office London Directory* for the census year is more realistic, with a list of 1,116 names and addresses in the central area and 650 in the suburbs, totalling 1,766. A cautionary note says 'see also architects, bricklayers, carpenters and surveyors'. The appellation 'builder' remains still somewhat ambiguous, however, because of the varieties of function performed, ranging from the smallest-scale suburban land development at one end to public works contracting at the other. The people I would like to identify here are the contracting builders who were responsible for public buildings and churches, commercial and domestic buildings in the City and central area generally.

Who were they? There are several ways of finding out. The main source I have used is the series of lists of competitive tenders published regularly in the building journals.[7] These cover only a small proportion of the construction activity proceeding in London at the period but they reflect, however imperfectly, that sector where architects were extracting from the building industry fair market prices for their clients' projects, a sector moreover in which builders had to be continuously competing to keep their businesses going.

If we take one year (1861) of the London tenders printed in the *Builder* we find 540 builders tendering for 263 works ranging in cost from a workhouse at £30,000 to alteration jobs at £100. An analysis of the lists gives the names of builders tendering for the largest-scale work and we find that of our 540 builders only 39 tendered for work over £10,000. Of these 39, only 7 tendered for more than one such contract in the year. We may reasonably suppose that these seven were among the largest and most active businesses at the moment. They were: Mansfield, Myers, Willson, Lawrence, Kirk and Parry, Hill Keddle and Lucas. Obviously if our analysis were carried through the whole ten years other names would come to the top while some of the seven would go down. A less laborious way of extracting the important names for the decade is by analysing a list of all those who built buildings sufficiently large or interesting to be illustrated either in the building journals, the *Illustrated London News* or the *Companion to the Almanac*. In this process Myers, Lucas and Dove Brothers come out top while all the other five in our previous list come in the first eighteen.

Yet another way of probing the building world of the sixties is to look at such records as can be found of builders' organizations. The London Builders Society was founded by a group of seventeen builders in 1834, with the object of protecting themselves against bad contracting pro-cedures and the arrogance of the architect (the RIBA was founded in the very same year!).[8] Later they had to defend themselves from another quarter – trade unionism – and by 1860 they had brought the Central Association of Master Builders into existence.[9] In 1859 the membership of the Society was 'sixty or seventy', in 1867 it was seventy-six.[10] Perhaps that was roughly the number of top-ranking firms in the ten years with which we are concerned. The leaders of the Society, as also of the allied Builders Benevolent Institution, include several of the names already mentioned, notably Myers, Lucas and Lawrence.[11]

What do we know about these people? Very little. Nobody has ever written about them and their biographies and business methods have, by now, become almost impenetrably obscure. *The Dictionary of National Biography* gives only the giants of the contracting world. Thomas Cubitt is there, of course, but he died five years before our decade opens, while his brother William, having retired in 1854, had moved into public life, becoming Lord Mayor in 1860 and 1861. The contracting firm continued under his name. Samuel Morton Peto is there but his wealth and fame depended more on vast railway constructions all over the world than on the building contracting which engaged him in London during the 1840s. He, like Thomas Brassey, and a few others belonged to the heroic class of Victorian contractor, the class to which Trollope's un-happy Sir Roger Scatcherd also belonged. The fact is that the mid-Victorian builders of our city streets are, historically speaking, a lost tribe.

However, we can ask general questions and partly answer them. The type of builder we are dealing with was in a fairly exclusive minority. In the great mob of London builders the commonest was the builder employing up to ten men and capable of nothing much more than putting in a shop-front.[12] Above him there were firms of all sizes and, in the top layer only, those which were general contractors in the sense which Thomas Cubitt had pioneered as long ago as the 1820s.[13] That is to say, businesses which incorporated all the trades, each trade con-ducted by its own foreman. These firms contracted in gross. In principle, there was no subletting, a practice frowned upon by architects as leading to irresponsible cut-price workmanship, though separate contracts were made for such things as gas-lighting, heating and often for ornamental carving.

Building was, in the sixties, London's biggest industry and these all-in contractors required large premises with good communications, a plentiful supply of labour and a continuous flow of work.[14] As to premises, some of the builders had their yard and offices in the same place and perhaps even lived on the spot; others had a business address in central London, a yard or yards elsewhere, and resided in the suburbs. Water transport was important, if not vital, to a big building concern. Myers established himself in Belvedere Road on the south bank in 1848. In 1853 Lucas Brothers arrived next door. By 1861, Richard Holland and Benjamin Hannen were there, too, with Lawrences just down the road at Pitfield Wharf where the National Theatre now stands. Cubitts had, besides their Gray's Inn Road works, a large establishment at the Isle of Dogs.[15] Builders in Islington like Dove Brothers of Studd Street and Hill of Charlton Place (who became Higgs and Hill) no doubt used the Regent's Canal.

A basic need for the almost wholly unmechanized industry of the sixties was a large labour force. It is hard to ascertain precisely what numbers these firms employed, for the obvious reason that there was continual fluctuation, labourers, bricklayers and carpenters being taken on and laid off as the work required them.[16] We hear of Myers employing two thousand men when he had to face a serious strike in 1851 and he cannot have been employing less than that number in the sixties when he was among the two or three busiest builders in London.[17] Cubitts were said to be employing three thousand men in 1876 and for them, too, the sixties had been a busy period.[18] These round figures are presumably rough assessments of the labour force at work at a given moment and it is interesting that when Benjamin Dixon Dove, senior partner in Dove Brothers, filled in his census return in 1861 he stated (quite gratuitously) that he employed 210 men and 11 boys.[19] These very precise figures possibly represent a cadre of workmen continuously employed at the Islington works.

Most essential of all to the big builder was a continuous flow of work and this was obtained almost entirely by competitive tendering all the year round. The system was an old one but by the sixties had reached a fierce intensity which is reflected in the published lists. In the *Builder*'s lists of a typical year (1865) we find Myers tendering for forty-four contracts, with only five (presumed) successes; Dove Brothers for twenty-four contracts, with three successes and Piper and Wheeler, a firm of comparable standing, for thirty-one contracts with no successes at all. The estimating clerks must have been under continuous pressure to catch enough acceptances to keep the business afloat without inviting disaster by under-pricing – a practice all too common in the lower ranks of the industry as a last gamble under impending bankruptcy.

The tendering system is one of the vital features in the Victorian building scene, a touchstone of change not only in building but in architecture, and for this reason. No reputable builder would tender unless quantities were supplied by a recognized quantity surveyor.[20] The taking out of quantities required very full working-drawings and specifications from the architect who would thus need to take on clerks (or 'assistants' as they preferred to be called)[21] for the purpose. This kind of employment contributed to the inflation of the architectural profession in the fifties and sixties and tended to create a 'lower deck' of professionalism, partly an 'under-dog' breed of limited but useful competence and partly a class of hopefuls who would very likely join the Architectural Association, debate about styles and clamour for professional qualifications and the regulation of competitions. As building became more an industry than a trade, so architecture became more a business than a profession. As the big builders killed the master-craftsman by absorbing him into industry, so the relations between architect and builder became as faceless as a deed of contract. The 'art action', as H. Bruce Allen put it in 1865, became 'wholly expended on paper'.[22]

The builder's business was always economically hazardous but whereas bankruptcies were commonplace in the middle and lower reaches, the big building firms seem rarely to have crashed. The spectacular failure of Peto and Betts in 1866 was within the larger contracting world of docks and railways. In the troubled seventies builders tended to merge with one another and often settled down to a hundred years of thriving existence. It is impressive to find how many of the great building names of the sixties are still current today. Concerning the founders and heads of the firms it is difficult to find much information. Obituary notices of builders, unlike those of architects, are rare and brief. One indubitable fact is that the big builder's business was conducted with ruthless efficiency. Notices of builders rarely fail to pay tribute to 'perseverance and strict integrity' – certainly true of the best.[23] If they add that the deceased had 'the welfare of his men at heart', this may have been true up to a point; but even the heartiest sense of workers' welfare would vanish on the approach of strike action, as was cruelly demonstrated by the solidarity of London builders in the great lock-out of 1859 when the nine-hour movement was, for the time being, smashed and twenty-four thousand operatives were adrift on the London streets for eight weeks.[24] The Victorian builder was tough. He was no remote board-room personage. If he was to survive he had to face his men, command them and, if necessary, endure their hatred.

If we think of the Thomas Cubitt generation as the first generation of great general contractors, most, though not all, of the builders of the sixties were second-generation men. George Myers, as it happens, was not. As he was perhaps the most conspicuous London builder of the sixties his story, or such little as I have gathered for this occasion, is of some interest here. Born in Hull in or about 1804[25] he was working as a mason in Beverley when Pugin visited there, probably in the early thirties. A pleasant anecdote comes in here. He helped Pugin with tackle to reach inaccessible parts of the Minster which Pugin was studying and was caught by his Gothic enthusiasm. By 1837 Myers was in business as a builder. He tendered for the new Catholic church at Derby without realizing that the architect was the young man he had helped at Beverley. Pugin recognized and embraced him and a long association followed. By 1844 Myers was established in Lambeth, where he gathered together a group of competent carvers, provided casts for study and was, according to Ferrey (who may exaggerate a little), responsible for the availability of so many good carvers at the period.[26] But Myers's building activities embraced every size, type and style. Two of his sons came into the business, which flourished at Ordnance Wharf, Belvedere Road till the father's death in 1875, when they disposed of it. Myers lived in modest affluence in the Clapham Road and left a comfortable but not spectacular fortune of £40,000.[27]

The story of Lucas Brothers also has provincial origins but begins later and runs what we may think a more spectacularly Victorian course. Charles, born in 1822, set up in business at Norwich, then joined his younger brother Thomas in developing an establishment at Lowestoft. Both brothers were on the staff of Samuel Morton Peto during his London contracting years. When Peto moved on to bigger things in 1847 the Lucas brothers took over his London business and built, among other things, two of Sir Charles Barry's great houses and his son's Covent Garden Theatre. The fifties and sixties were the firm's great London period. With John Kelk they were responsible for the International Exhibition of 1862.[28] Later they had a big share of the underground railway work in which the elder John Aird was involved and with him they carried out the District Line.[29] In 1870 they went into business with the younger Aird and formed three separate firms, one of which, Lucas and Aird, built the Royal Albert Docks.[30] Thus, the Lucases, like Peto before them, moved into the wider field of public works contracting and became immensely rich. Charles left £300,000 at his death in 1895. Thomas was made a baronet and died in 1902, worth £750,000.[31] That sort of money was not made out of building banks, warehouses and model dwellings.

Dove Brothers of Islington came up at the same time as the Lucases but never issued into the more ambitious fields of contracting. There seem originally to have been four brothers but one dropped out and a formal partnership of three brothers was made in 1862.[32] Throughout the fifties Doves were tendering, mainly for churches, chapels and schools, and from the first they seem to have specialized, as they still do, in these types. In the sixties they certainly built more churches and chapels than any other contractor. No fortunes were made and throughout our period the head of the firm lived modestly at the yard in Islington.

These three builders stand at the top of my list of those whose performances were most frequently illustrated. It may well be that Doves owe their position to the fact that churches make better illustrative material than some other things. There are big names further down the list – the firm of Lawrence, for instance, which had a solid City background, the founder being an Alderman in 1848 and his two sons, James and William, becoming Lords Mayor in 1860 and 1868 respectively, with a baronetcy for James in 1869. The Cubitt contracting firm, William Cubitt and Co., stands high and so does that of Piper and Wheeler. Thomas Piper, a second-generation builder (his father had been Mason to the City), was conspicuously one of the aristocrats of the building world, with intellectual and institutional interests of a distinguished kind. He retired in 1867 and when he died in 1873 his obituarist noted significantly that it would be 'not uninstructive to examine into the reasons why he did not, like some of his contemporaries, make a large fortune as a contractor'.[33] As we learn from Piper's evidence before the Royal Commission on Trades Unions of 1867, his attitude to labour was hard. But perhaps not hard enough.[34]

I have not attempted to discover the historic roots of other great contractors of the sixties. It would be a worthwhile exercise and there is a field for research here where one would like to see things done, following the lead given by Hermione Hobhouse with her book on Cubitt.

Very different from the contracting builders we have been considering were those who were primarily estate developers but using their own labour. Thomas Cubitt had set two patterns for adventurous builders – the all-in contracting pattern and the speculative development pattern. Both were followed, but never again to any considerable extent, by a single-family concern. As with the contractors, our present ignorance of the developers is profound. What, for instance, do we know of the virtual creators of the South Kensington area in and around the land acquired by the Commissioners for the Great Exhibition in 1852 – C. J. Freake, Charles Aldin and Thomas Jackson? I ask this question in anticipation that the later Kensington volumes of the *Survey of London*, under Dr Shepherd's editorship, will tell us a good deal. Their initiatives, which probably owe much to what they learnt from Cubitt, mostly belong to the fifties and so hardly concern us here. But they flourished through the sixties and Freake, anyway, became rich, got his baronetcy in 1882 and died in 1884. Freake was what we would call a developer but he certainly employed his own labour, for we hear of him prosecuting three of his labourers for intimidating men who accepted a wage rate which the three had rejected. The magistrate let them off with three months' hard labour and a warning.[35] The *Times* obituary of Sir Charles Freake is disappointing. Nothing is said of building South Kensington and the points made are that he married the sister of a Brigadier-General and that his daughter-in-law was a great-grand-daughter of the sixth Earl of Lauderdale.[36] As Freake started at the bottom his social climbing was certainly an achievement but unfortunately it is not what interests posterity. One has the impression that a career in speculative building, however successful, was not a thing to be much doted on when a man had come through it and out at the top.

The generally, though not universally odious reputation of building developers comes out in the *Builder's* obituary of John Spicer who operated through the sixties on the Gunter estate in Earl's Court. He was, says the editor, 'one of the class of conscientious builders that we have known and still know despite the popular idea that nothing but shiftiness and chicanery are to be found in the calling'.[37] The editor, George Godwin, was, as it happens, the surveyor to the Gunter estate and thus had a rather special relationship with the builders there. Godwin also reports approvingly of work proceeding on the adjoining Radcliffe estate where Corbett and McClymont had built 550 houses by 1868, a massive accretion to London of the sixties, with 400 more houses to come. They were using mass-production techniques of some interest, the planing, mortising, tenoning, tonguing and grooving of their joinery being mechanically operated.[38] This sounds like the sort of mechanization which, as Miss Hobhouse tells us, William Cubitt and Co. had been operating at their Isle of Dogs works many years earlier.[39] Here, as so often in the study of the Victorian building world, one finds that innovations in organization, technology and even design must be credited to the Cubitts.

If South Kensington building history remains for the present twilit, the same cannot be said for that of North Kensington, now irradiated with formidable intensity by the *Survey of London's* thirty-seventh volume.[40] If time allowed I would steal extensively from this work. I will allow myself one allusion, which is to the performance, through the fifties and sixties, of the Radford brothers in Pembridge Square and Holland Park. The Radfords, who came from Devon, were, it seems, prudent and respectable. They employed about sixty men. Their houses – some two hundred in all – were nearly all of one design,

Francis Radford's: a design of the supercharged mannerist variety once thought disgraceful but now loved for its very ostentation. They are excellently built and the Radfords, who financed themselves by a long series of mortgages, arranged by attorneys, got reasonably and deservedly rich. For the story in detail and for others no less relevant to London of the sixties I refer you to the *Survey* volume, where you will find not only the best insights to date into the mechanics of London development but superb measured drawings and a galaxy of photo-graphs.

Estate development and building in the outer suburbs I deliberately exclude from this paper. Professor Dyos of Leicester has opened up this huge and complex area of study, notably in his book on Camberwell of 1961, and it is a pleasure, in passing, to pay him tribute.[41]

It is time to leave the contractors and developers and look at the other major component of the building world, the architects. The architec-tural profession increased rapidly in the early Victorian decades. Robert Kerr, at an RIBA conference in 1874, observed that 'where there was one architect of fair pretensions half a century ago [i.e. 1825], there are at this moment literally twenty at the very least'.[42] This was not a bad guess. It presupposes a rate of increase of nearly four hundred in every decade. The national census increases in the decades 1851–61 and 1861–71 average out at almost precisely that. Admittedly the three previous decades, for which there are no figures, must reduce this but not, perhaps, by very much. If we can trust the census figures for rela-tive increases we cannot take their numerical totals as realistic, but here again Kelly's directories come to our rescue. In 1861, Kelly prints the names and addresses of 638 London architects and most consider-ately gives, by a system of symbols, an indication of those who called themselves architects *and surveyors*. This category constitutes over half the total, which seems to show that the increase in the profession was, as one would expect from what I said earlier, on the bread-and-butter rather than the aesthetic side. A number of these 'architects and surveyors' would be quantity surveyors, a profession which sprang out of the side of architecture under the pressure of the competitive tender-ing system, and obtained a standing of its own. Kelly also indicates which of the listed architects are fellows or associates of the Institute of British Architects. They number 209, or rather less than a third of the total and include most of the familiar mid-Victorian names. It must be added that Kelly's list of 'surveyors', as distinct from 'architects and surveyors', totals only 210 and covers a whole variety of functions such as land and estate agency, auctioneering and land surveying and is only remotely connected with our theme.

The RIBA in the sixties was a strong and distinguished institution, entry to which was by election after seven years in practice, and election to which was esteemed something of an honour, exceeded only by election to the Royal Academy, to which body only three architects were elected between 1847 and 1870. The Institute occupied beautiful eighteenth-century rooms in Lord Macclesfield's old house in Conduit Street with a salaried secretary and already a fine library and was permitted to be the 'Royal' Institute from 1866. Its presidents in the sixties were Cockerell, Tite, Donaldson, Beresford Hope and Tite again – men of considerable influence and, in two cases, of great wealth, but singularly different in personality and performance. Nor did they quite belong to our period. Cockerell, Tite and Donaldson were really early and not mid Victorians and the rising men in the Institute in the sixties were George Gilbert Scott, M.D. and T.H. Wyatt and the younger Charles Barry. The RIBA was remarkable for a lively catholicity; it retained what one might call a 'literary and philosophical' character and the papers read shew a consistent balance between archaeology, science, professional practice and fine art.[43] The intellectual side of the Institute at this time is reflected in that noble achievement of eclectic scholarship, the Architectural Publication Society's *Dictionary*, which was being edited all through the sixties from Conduit Street by Wyatt Papworth.

With seven years in practice as a qualification for election, the RIBA membership was fairly mature. Sheltering under the same Conduit Street roof, however, at a nominal rent, was a junior and wholly independent body, the Architectural Association. Founded by some rebellious youngsters in 1847, it was in low water when it began to use the Conduit Street building for its meetings but it quickly revived under a succession of notable young presidents, A. W. Blomfield and R. W. Edis especially, who contributed significantly to the London architecture of the sixties and beyond. Primarily, the AA was a self-help society, meeting once a fortnight for a design class and in alternate weeks for papers and discussions. Its membership of about two hundred, rising to nearly five hundred by 1809, came from the clerks and articled pupils who wanted more from architecture than a mere living. They wanted formal education and they wanted a properly regulated competition system and on both these issues they were able to give occasional prods to the senior body.[44] As a result the RIBA held the first voluntary examination in 1863: it was not a great success because it conferred neither membership nor anything else, but it was a signpost.[45] On the competition question the RIBA held debates but many years elapsed before it acquired the monopolistic authority which could dictate reforms.

The architectural profession in the sixties was a gentleman's profession – but only just. The RIBA upheld the tradition of the gentleman architect inherited from Sir William Chambers and maintained through the years by an irreproachable élite. But the recruitment in the thirties, forties and fifties had a decidedly 'lower middle' tone. Never do we find sons of the gentry entering architecture as they did the Church or the Law, or even the fine arts. To a great extent the expanding profession was recruited from its own sphere of activity. Some of the top architects of the sixties came from honoured architectural dynasties, such as the Wyatts and the Hardwicks. The sons and pupils of Sir Charles Barry and Professor Cockerell distinguished themselves. At a lower level, many practitioners of the sixties had architectural, surveying or building backgrounds going back two generations, while at a lower level still, the sons of builders and builders' tradesmen, looking for a more genteel career than their fathers, helped to swell the ranks.[46] From outside, sons of clergy, like Scott, or of small solicitors, like Street, represent the social high-water mark. They were an important infusion, uninhibited by paternal tradition and happy to be innovators.

The architect's education, through articled pupilage, was, in the 1860s, becoming less and less satisfactory for the simple reason that, with the increasing drudgery involved in practice, pupils tended to be used as junior clerks and to spend their time tracing, copying or doing repetitive operations on standard products.[47] After pupilage, opportunity was sought either through social contacts, obtained very often by deliberate touting, or through competitions, but far more through the first than through the second. Open competitions, mostly initiated in the provinces, were a mere gamble, usually for dubious rewards, and only very young architects with time on their hands went in for them. The more promising competitions were mostly limited by invitation to a few architects of mature experience.

I can find no adequate method of representing the pattern of employment of London's six hundred architects. The prevailing type was the general practitioner who dealt confidently with any and every sort of building, though sometimes finding peculiarly fruitful patronage in a particular group or persuasion or by virtue of a surveyor-ship to some corporate body. A class of middling successful London architect can perhaps be identified by listing those who were elected to the District Surveyorships under the Building Act of 1844 and the Metropolis Management Act of 1855.[48] They were men in private practice who, after submitting to an examination, were authorized to collect fees for passing plans submitted by other architects for buildings in their allotted districts. In 1860 there were fifty-six of these officers covering the metropolitan area and the names of many are well known. Though never quite of the top rank, they form a representative body of acknowledged professional competence which the architectural his-torian should not overlook. These Surveyorships were much sought after so long as it was permissible to combine them with private practice; when that permission was withdrawn in 1891 nobody wanted them. The important districts brought in well over £1,000 a year in fees and the office carried a status which attracted clients. In the City, to take two examples, John Young and Edmund Woodthorpe, District Surveyors for the east and north divisions respectively, had conspicuously fine office and warehouse practices. Woodthorpe had the Surveyorship of Spitalfields into the bargain and was, in addition, Surveyor to the Girdlers' Company and to the Parish of St Giles

Cripplegate: a combination representing a typically prosperous City practice.[49] John Young had probably the biggest warehouse practice of the time.[50] Outside the City and in the suburbs it is noticeable that substantial commissions accrued to District Surveyors. How, otherwise, did the relatively obscure F. W. Porter,[51] District Surveyor for Holborn and East Strand, come to build the magnificent £30,000 London County Bank in Chancery Lane; or Henry Jarvis[52] to be so busy with churches and houses and a vestry hall in Camberwell as well as having a good warehouse practice in the central area?

Office holding without facilities for private practice was, in general, a sad affair. The Metropolitan Board of Works, to whom the District Surveyors were responsible, had its own full-time Superintending Architect. The first to be appointed, in 1855, was Frederick Marrables who designed the Board's offices in Spring Gardens (recently destroyed) but was so overloaded with report-writing that he resigned after five years, though offered a 25 per cent rise in salary.[53] He was succeeded by George Vulliamy, the designer of the architectural parts of the Victoria Embankment including the famous lamps; he survived till his health failed in 1886.[54] In the City of London the ancient office of Clerk-of-the-Works (which became 'Architect' in 1847) was held by James Bunstone Bunning whose performance in the previous seventeen years had included such outstanding things as the Coal Exchange and the Metropolitan Cattle Market. But, grossly overworked and already consumptive, he collapsed on the steps of the Mansion House in 1863 and died soon afterwards.[55] The short list for his successor was, understandably perhaps, not very brilliant and the office went to the genial and portly Horace Jones, a man of tougher fibre but less talent.[56]

At Her Majesty's Office of Works, the position of the official architect was a sad one in another way. James Pennethorne, Nash's professional legatee and a designer of immense ability, had, after serving with Works and with Woods and Forests for many years, been given the title of 'Salaried Architect and Surveyor' to the Office in 1859. He was allowed to design such government buildings as were not handed out to private architects by competition or otherwise and he did achieve the remarkable London University building in Burlington Gardens.

But in 1869, the First Commissioner, Sir Henry Layard, found the office of Salaried Architect otiose and retired Pennethorne with a knighthood and a pension.[57] After which the Office of Works sank very low.

The mid-Victorian hatred of official architecture and, indeed, the fear of seeing public money spent on architecture at all, was at its height in the sixties. We see it at its most intense in the conditions for some of the competitions arising out of the provisions of the Metropolitan Poor Act of 1867. In those for the Poplar and Stepney Sick Asylum, for instance, it was specifically provided that designs should possess 'no architectural pretensions whatever'. It is not unamusing that one of the unsuccessful competitors on that occasion was young George Gilbert Scott, Sir Gilbert's brilliant son – evidently trying his luck with Poor Law work as his father had done a generation earlier.[58]

What emerges from this brief consideration of office-holding architects is, of course, that nearly all the major architectural opportunities and achievements, all the glory and much of the profit is associated with the private practitioners. These I find impossible to set in any sort of order unless by their artistic parentage and stylistic affiliation. With categories of this kind we find ourselves on the threshold of art history, an area which on this occasion I want at all costs to avoid. I would like to conclude, however, with some visual evidence and of this I have made a rather frivolously controlled selection. Having compiled a list of illustrated buildings with a view to identifying the leading builders I thought it might be instructive to discover which architects came out top under the same test. You may care to hazard your own guess as to who was the most illustrated London architect of the 1860s. You will probably say Sir Gilbert Scott and I cannot seriously dispute this though in my count E. M. Barry does get one nominal point over him. In a total of 160 architects of illustrated London buildings, 17 earn more than three points. After Barry and Scott they are: Alfred Darbishire, G. Somers Clarke, the brothers Francis, James Murray, Horace Jones, John Giles (with or without partner), John Tarring, Francis Fowke, A. W. Blomfield, Henry Jarvis, John Taylor, J. T. Knowles (senior and junior), Bassett Keeling, John Johnson and C. G. Searle.

I am not inviting you to take this list very seriously but it does happen that by shuffling the illustrated works of these masters and rearranging them typologically a representative picture emerges of what was happening in the London building world of the 1860s.

You will have perceived by now that what I have been doing is to take a small slice of architectural history, stand it on its head and see what falls out. What, in fact, has fallen out? Almost everything, you may say, which, in the history of art, really matters. I have made no mention of London buildings by Butterfield, Street, Pearson, Burges, Waterhouse, Philip Webb or half a dozen other celebrities whom you could name. I did not exclude them on purpose, but my method of approach did not seem to require their presence. If an apology is required it is simply this. I believe that an architectural historian should, from time to time, look over the shoulders and under the feet of the conventionally accepted heroes and try to see what went on around them and on what they stood; and, furthermore, to see whether that hinterland may not contain some very adequate heroes of its own. This is what, in my brief excursion into London's building history, I have tried to do.

OFFICES

2 General Credit and Discount Co., Lothbury (as first proposed). Architect: G. Somers Clarke. Builders: Lucas Bros.

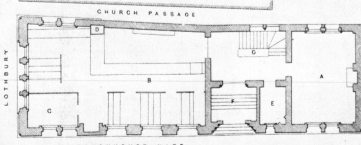

CHURCH PASSAGE

LOTHBURY

TOKENHOUSE YARD

Reference.

A . Discount Managers Room.
B . Discount Department.
C . Head Clerk's Office.
D . Lift.
E . Porter.
F . Lobby.
G . Staircase.

2

OFFICES FOR
LETTING

3 City Offices Co.,
Lombard Street.
Architects: F. and H.
Francis. Builders:
Myers. Cost: £70,000.

4 Offices in Old Broad
Street and Bishopsgate.
Architects: F. and H.
Francis. Builders:
David King and Sons.
Cost: £80,000.
Demolished.

5 Offices and warehouse,
Great Tower Street.
Architects: Finch, Hill
and Paraire. Builders:
Hill and Sons.
Demolished.

6

7

6 Pocock Bros., leather merchants, Southwark Bridge Road. Architect: Henry Jarvis. Builder: Henshaw. Cost: £4,800. *Demolished.*

7 Lewis and Allenby, silk merchants, Conduit Street. Architect: James Murray. Builders: Lucas Bros.

8 FLOWER MARKET: the Floral Hall, Covent Garden. Architect: E. M. Barry. Builders: Lucas Bros. Iron and glass: H. Grissell.

9

10

11

9 AUCTION ROOMS: the Auction Mart, Tokenhouse Yard. Architect: G. Somers Clarke. Builders: Lucas Bros. *Demolished.*

10 SHOP PREMISES in Oxford Street for Hyam and Co., manufacturing clothiers. Architect: Horace Jones. Lowest tender: Pritchard, £9,000. *Demolished.*

11 STAINED GLASS WORKS for Heaton, Butler and Baynes, King Street, Covent Garden. Architect: A. W. Blomfield. Builder: Howard of Covent Garden.

12 PRINTING WORKS for the Printing and Publishing Co., West Smithfield. Architect: G. Somers Clarke. Builders: Kirk and Parry. *Demolished.*

13 SUBWAY at the high-level station, Crystal Palace. Architect: E. M. Barry. Builders: Lucas Bros. Cost: £100,000.

14 STATION: Herne Hill; for the London, Chatham and Dover Railway Co. Architect: John Taylor, Jun.

15 BRIDGE across Ludgate Hill, for the London, Chatham and Dover Railway Co. Architect: John Taylor, Jun. Engineers: Joseph Cubitt and F. T. Turner. *Much altered.*

13

14

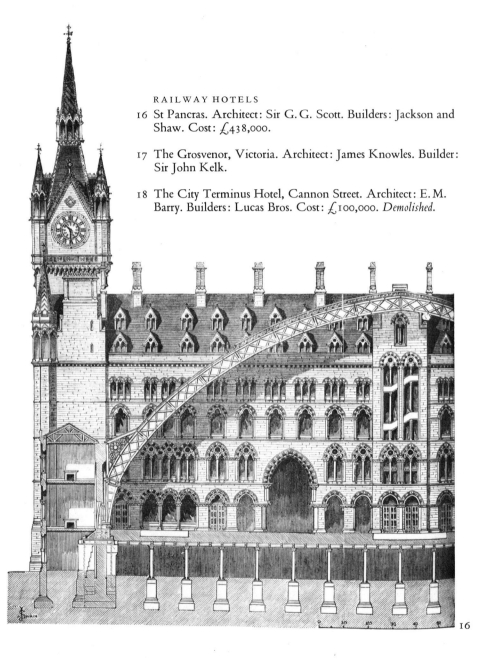

RAILWAY HOTELS

16 St Pancras. Architect: Sir G. G. Scott. Builders: Jackson and Shaw. Cost: £438,000.

17 The Grosvenor, Victoria. Architect: James Knowles. Builder: Sir John Kelk.

18 The City Terminus Hotel, Cannon Street. Architect: E. M. Barry. Builders: Lucas Bros. Cost: £100,000. *Demolished.*

17

18

19

20

19 The Langham, Portland Place. Architect: John Giles. Builders: Lucas Bros.

20 The Palace Hotel, Buckingham Gate. Architect: James Murray. Builders: Lucas Bros.

21 TURKISH BATHS, Jermyn Street. Architect: G. Somers Clarke. Cost: £6,000. *Demolished.*

22 The Philharmonic Hall,
Islington. Architects: Finch,
Hill and Paraire. Builders:
Holland and Hannen.

23 The New Surrey Theatre,
Blackfriars Road. Architect:
John Ellis. Builder: C.M.
Foster. *Demolished.*

24 The Strand Music Hall.
Architect: Bassett Keeling.
Builder: Trollope.
Demolished.

25 St George's Hall, Langham
Place. Architect: John
Taylor, Jun. *Demolished.*

22

23

24

25

26 MANSION for Sir S. Morton Peto, Kensington Palace Gardens. Architect: James Murray. Builders: Lucas Bros. Cost: £45,000–£50,000.

26

TERRACE HOUSES

27 1–4 Hyde Park Gate. Architect: J. Tarring. Developer and builder: William Jackson.

28 Cedars Estate, Clapham Common. Architect: James Knowles. Developer and builder: Henry Harris.

27

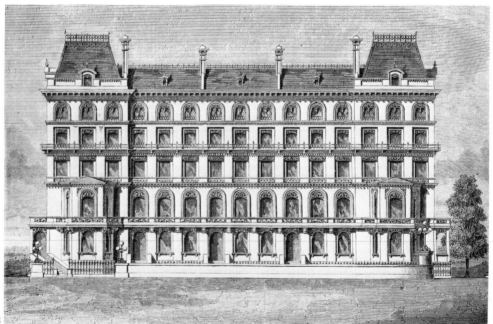

28

29 HOUSE, 'Torwood',
Wimbledon, for W.
Edgcumbe Rendle.
Architect: John Giles.
Cost: £5,000
(exclusive of billiard-
room and
conservatory).
Demolished.

30 SEMI-DETACHED
HOUSES, Peckham
Rye. Architect: Henry
Jarvis. Builder:
Henshaw. Cost
£2,000. *Demolished.*

32

31 CHAMBERS for letting, Chancery Lane. Architect: A. W. Blomfield. Builders: Brown and Robinson.

32 CLUB-HOUSE: Thatched House (now Constitutional) Club, St James's Street. Architect: James Knowles. Builders: George Smith and Co.

B. SLY DEL.   T. HEAVISIDE 33

33 St Mary Abbots, Kensington. Architect: Sir
G. G. Scott. Builders: Dove Bros. Cost:
£8,375, without tower.

34 St Paul, Haggerston. Architect: A. W.
Blomfield. Builders: Holland and Hannen.
Cost: £6,000. *Demolished.*

35 St Clement, Barnsbury. Architect: Sir G. G.
Scott. Builders: Dove Bros. Cost: £7,000.

35

34

36 MISSION HOUSE, Bedfordbury, St Martin-
in-the-Fields. Architect: A. W. Blomfield.
Builders: Child, Son and Martin. Cost:
£2,300. *Demolished.*

CHAPELS

37 Wesleyan Chapel, Mostyn Road, Brixton. Architect: J. Tarring and Son. Builders: Myers and Sons. Cost: £6,760.

38 Baptist and Independent Chapel, Hampstead. Architect: C. G. Searle. Builder: William Hill. Cost: £5,000.

39 SCHOOL: St Giles' National School, Endell Street. Architect: E. M. Barry. Builders: Mansfield and Son.

39

40 MARKET (philanthropic enterprise): Columbia Market. Architect: H. A. Darbishire. Builders: Cubitt and Co. *Demolished.*

41 ASYLUM for Merchant Seamen's Orphans, Snaresbrook (now Wanstead Hospital). Architect: G. Somers Clarke. Builders: Kirk and Parry.

42 HOUSING (philanthropic enterprise): Peabody Square, Westminster. Architect:
H. A. Darbishire. Builders: W. Cubitt and Co. *Demolished.*

43 HOUSING (civic): Corporation Buildings, Farringdon Road. Architect: Horace
Jones. Cost: £37,000. *Demolished.*

44 HOUSING (investment): Model Dwellings, The Mall, Kensington. Architect: James Murray. Builders: Lucas Bros.

PUBLIC WORKS

45 Vestry-hall of St Mary's, Newington. Architect: Henry Jarvis. Builders: Piper and Wheeler. Cost: £10,000.

46 Public offices and vestry-hall, West Ham Local Board of Health, Stratford. Architects: John Giles and Lewis Angell.

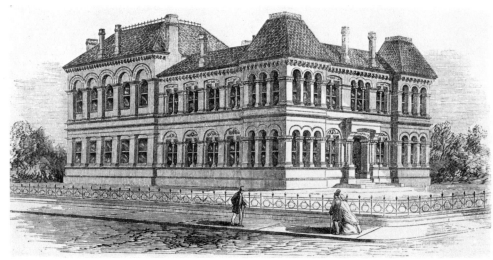

47

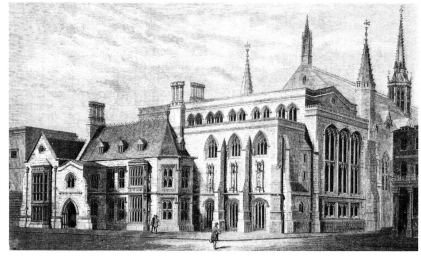

48

PUBLIC WORKS

47 Metropolitan Meat Market, Smithfield. Architect: Horace Jones. Builders: Brown and Robinson. Cost: £134,460. ˙

48 Guildhall Library and Museum. Architect: Horace Jones. Builder: Trollope. Cost: £21,360.

49 St Pancras Infirmary (for Board of Guardians), now part of Whittington Hospital. Architects: John Giles and Biven. Builder: Henshaw. Cost: £36,000.

49

PUBLIC WORKS

50 Courtyard of the South Kensington Museum (now the Victoria and Albert).
Architect: Francis Fowke. Builders: Smith and Taylor.

51 International Exhibition Building, 1862. Architect: Francis Fowke. Builders:
Kelk and Lucas. *Demolished.*

PUBLIC WORKS

52 Foreign and India Offices, Whitehall. Architects: Sir G. G. Scott and Sir M. D. Wyatt. Builders: Smith and Taylor. Cost: £500,000.

53 The Albert Memorial. Architect: Sir
G. G. Scott. Builder: Sir John Kelk.
Cost: over £120,000.

NOTES

1 *Illustrated London News*, 1860, 1, p. 229.
2 GLC Record Office, County Hall: MBW 1,772, 1,773, 1,774. The peak year was 1868, when fees were received in respect of 8,863 new buildings.
3 T. C. Barker and M. Robbins, *A History of London Transport*, 1 (the nineteenth century), 1963.
4 *Accounts and Papers, 1863*, LIII, pt. 1, p. 391.
5 *Ibid.*, p. 394.
6 *Accounts and Papers, 1873*, LXXI, pt. i, p. xl.
7 The practice of publishing tenders started in the *Builder* in 1845, with the object of exposing careless or dishonest estimating by builders leading to wild variations in prices. The lists were sent in by architects and were perhaps solicited, though there was also the incentive of self-advertisement.
8 *Builder,* 1860, p. 109.
9 R. W. Postgate, *The Builder's History* (1923), p. 197.
10 *Report of the Royal Commission on Trade Unions,* 1867, P.P. 1867, XXXII, p. 105.
11 The *Builder* contains periodical reports on the Builders Benevolent Institution. See especially 1861, p. 740, for report of annual dinner at which the Lord Mayor, William Cubitt, presided.
12 *Building News,* 1866, p. 87, mentions the small builder, employing not more than six men, 'whose largest jobs are only shop-fronts'. The census returns for 1851 show that at that date more builders employed ten men than any other number. *Accounts and Papers, 1852–3,* LXXXVIII, pt. 1, p.28.
13 H. Hobhouse, *Thomas Cubitt, master-builder* (1971), Chap. 2. E. W. Cooney, 'The Origins of the Victorian Master Builders', *Economic History Review*, ser. 2, VIII (1955–6), pp. 167–76.
14 See the account of the London building industry in F. Sheppard, *London 1808–70: the Infernal Wen* (1971), pp. 95–101.
15 Hobhouse, *op. cit.,* p. 102.
16 Four or five hundred men digging foundations at the Foreign Office were 'discharged gradually as the work goes on'. *Report . . . Trades Unions, ut supra,* p. 107.
17 *Builder,* 1851, p. 734. The strike was for a short Saturday. Myers met five or six hundred of the men in discussion.
18 *Ibid.,* 1876, p. 211. This figure was stated in the account of a visit by the Architectural Association to the works in Gray's Inn Road.
19 Public Record Office, 1861 census returns, RG9/126, f. 62.
20 *Builder,* 1870, p. 831.
21 *Ibid.,* 1856, p. 31.
22 *Ibid.,* 1865, p. 32.
23 The quotations are from the obituary notice of William Higgs, *Builder,* 1883, 1, p. 93.

24 Postgate, *op. cit.*, p. 171.

25 Public Record Office, 1861 census returns, RG9/362, f. 17.

26 B. Ferrey, *Recollections of A.N.W. Pugin* (1861), pp. 185–6.

27 Will, Probate Registry, Somerset House. Among Myers's effects were 'a dining-room table designed by me', an ebony and painted cabinet representing the life of St Joseph, a portrait of himself and three other paintings, a drawing by him of the reredos as restored at Beverley Minster, the original drawing by Haag of the Medieval Court at the 1851 Exhibition, and various books, prints, drawings and manuscripts. Owen Jones's *Grammar of Ornament* and Myers's watch were itemized among bequests to the eldest son. Myers lived at 143 Clapham Road but the house has been demolished.

28 *Illustrated London News*, 10 May 1862, p. 481. *The Times*, 6 December 1895, p. 6, quoting *Sussex Daily News*. *Ibid.*, 8 March 1902, p. 9.

29 R. K. Middlemas, *The Master Builders* (1963), pp. 126–7.

30 *Ibid.*, pp. 130, 136.

31 Wills of Charles and Thomas Lucas, Probate Registry, Somerset House.

32 Will of Benjamin Dixon Dove, Probate Registry, Somerset House.

33 *Builder*, 1873, p. 651.

34 *Report . . . Trades Unions, ut supra*, p. 107.

35 *Builder*, 1857, p. 224.

36 *The Times*, 9 October 1884, p. 5, col. 6.

37 *Builder*, 1883, I, p. 93.

38 *Ibid.*, 1868, p. 201.

39 Hobhouse, *op. cit.*, Appendix 5, pp. 490–1.

40 Greater London Council, *Survey of London* (ed. F. H. W. Sheppard), XXXVII.

41 *Victorian Suburb: a Study of the Growth of Camberwell* (1961); 'The Speculative Builders and Developers of Victorian London', *Victorian Studies*, XI, supplement (1968).

42 *Builder*, 1874, p. 530.

43 There is no history of the RIBA. *The Growth and Work of the RIBA* (ed. J. A. Gotch, 1934) contains a historical sketch by the editor and other papers. See also C. L. Eastlake, 'An Historical Sketch of the Institute', *Trans. RIBA*, 1875–6, pp. 258 *et seq.*

44 J. Summerson, *The Architectural Association, 1847–1947*, 1947.

45 B. Kaye, *The Development of the Architectural Profession in Britain*, 1960.

46 Sir Gilbert Scott's account of his fellow pupils in Edmeston's office, which he entered in 1827, is relevant. G. G. Scott, *Personal and Professional Recollections*, 1879, pp. 57, 67.

47 A typical case is described in a letter to the *Builder*, 1858, pp. 214–15, of a youth who, being articled for five years at a premium of nearly £320, found himself 'placed exactly on a footing with salaried clerks and messengers'. On remonstrating, he was told that this treatment was 'customary in the profession'.

48 H. Lovegrove, *Some Account of the District Surveyors' Association of London* (Beckenham, 1915). C. C. Knowles and P. H. Pitt. *The History of Building Regulation in London 1189–1972*, 1972.

49 Obituary notice, *Builder*, 1887, II, p. 798.

50 Seventeen warehouses by him occur in the *Builder*'s lists of tenders between 1860 and 1868. Obituary notice, *Builder*, 1877, p. 328.

51 Obituary notice, *Builder*, 1901, II, p. 468.

52 Obituary notice, *Builder*, 1900, 1, p. 406.
53 *Builder*, 1861, p. 130.
54 Article in *The Dictionary of National Biography*.
55 Article in *The Dictionary of National Biography*.
56 Article in *The Dictionary of National Biography*.
57 For a good account of the administration of the Office of Works see article in *Builder*, 1877, pp. 897 et seq.
58 *Builder*, 1868, p. 827.

SOURCES OF ILLUSTRATIONS

1 Guildhall Library, City of London
2 *Building News*, 1868, p. 11
3 *The Illustrated London News*, 1868, ii, p. 105
4 *Building New*, 1867, p. 145
5 *Building News*, 1866, p. 832
6 *The Builder*, 1864, p. 315
7 *The Illustrated London News*, 1866, i, p. 360
8 *The Builder*, 1860, p. 89
9 *The Builder*, 1867, p. 891
10 *Building News*, 1863, p. 355
11 *Building News*, 1860, p. 895
12 *The Builder*, 1864, p. 901
13 *Building News*, 1863, p. 337
14 *The Illustrated London News*, 1865, ii, p. 304
15 *The Illustrated London News*, 1863, ii, p. 493
16 *Building News*, 1869, p. 136
17 *The Illustrated London News*, 1860, ii, p. 8
18 *The Builder*, 1866, p. 761
19 *The Builder*, 1863, p. 533
20 *The Illustrated London News*, 1861, i, p. 411
21 *The Illustrated London News*, 1862, ii, p. 96
22 *Building News*, 1866, p. 733
23 *The Illustrated London News*, 1866, i, p. 73
24 *Building News*, 1863, p. 869
25 *The Illustrated London News*, 1867, i, p. 649
26 *The Builder*, 1865, p. 677
27 *Building News*, 1860, p. 292
28 *The Builder*, 1860, p. 380
29 *The Builder*, 1865, p. 801
30 *Building News*, 1866, p. 762
31 *The Builder*, 1864, p. 901
32 *The Illustrated London News*, 1865, ii, p. 324
33 *The Builder*, 1870, p. 11
34 *The Builder*, 1860, p. 201
35 *Building News*, 1860, p. 607
36 *The Builder*, 1861, p. 807
37 *The Builder*, 1870, p. 146
38 *The Illustrated London News*, 1865, ii, p. 341
39 *The Builder*, 1860, p. 631
40 *The Builder*, 1869, p. 347
41 *Building News*, 1862, p. 337
42 *The Illustrated London News*, 1869, i, p. 317
43 *The Builder*, 1865, p. 485
44 *The Illustrated London News*, i, p. 89
45 *The Illustrated London News*, 1865, ii, p. 324
46 *Building News*, 1867, p. 885
47 *The Builder*, 1866, p. 957
48 *The Builder*, 1870, p. 687
49 *The Builder*, 1869, pp. 28/29
50 *The Builder*, 1870, p. 467
51 *The Builder*, 1861, p. 213
52 *The Illustrated London News*, 1866, ii, p. 341
53 *The Builder*, 1863, p. 371